JANUARY

THAW

University of Pittsburgh Press

January Thaw

Bruce Guernsey

Published by the University of Pittsburgh Press, Pittsburgh, Pa. 15260
Feffer and Simons, Inc., London
Manufactured in the United States of America

Library of Congress Cataloging in Publication Data

Guernsey, Bruce, 1944–
  January thaw.

  (Pitt poetry series)
  I. Title. II. Series.
PS3557.U33J3   811'.54   81-70219
ISBN 0-8229-3459-0   AACR2
ISBN 0-8229-5339-0 (pbk.)

Thanks are due to the Illinois Arts Council, a State Agency, whose support assisted the author in the writing of this book.

Acknowledgment is made to the following publications for permission to reprint some of the poems that appear in this book: *Ascent, Beloit Poetry Journal, Chowder Review, College English, Green House, Illinois Quarterly, Inlet, Jam To-Day, Lillabulero, Marilyn, Medical Opinion, Nantucket Review, Nebraska Review,* and *Xanadu.*

"The Dismal Swamp" and "The Lost Fisherman" originally appeared in *Apple.* "A Certain Providence" is reprinted from *The Atlantic Monthly,* copyright © 1977, by The Atlantic Monthly Company, Boston, Massachusetts. "Canoe," "The Apple," and "The Nest" are reprinted with permission from Blair & Ketchum's *Country Journal,* August 1980 and October 1981, copyright by Country Journal Publishing Co., Inc. "The Icehouse" first appeared in *The Nation,* copyright 1981 by The Nation Associates, Inc. "Back Road" was originally published in *Poetry,* copyright 1980 by The Modern Poetry Association. "Houses We Lived In" is reprinted from *Shenandoah:* The Washington and Lee University Review with the permission of the Editor, copyright Sept. 24, 1974 by Washington and Lee University. "Fishing the Newfound" is reprinted with permission from the August 1978 issue of *Yankee* Magazine, published by Yankee, Inc., Dublin, N. H., copyright 1978.

The publication of this book is supported by grants from the National Endowment for the Arts in Washington, D.C., a Federal agency, and the Pennsylvania Council on the Arts.

for my grandfather,

William H. Heffernan, 1883–1973

CONTENTS

Part One

A Winter Without Snow   3
Back Road   4
The Snow Man   5
Louis B. Russell   6
Stray   8
The Tongue   9
Toad   10
The Dump Pickers   11
The Apple   12
Splitting Wood   14
The Nest   15
Falling to Sleep   16
Flying Home   17

Part Two

The Bottle   23
The Affair   24
The Skull   25
Mug Shot   26
The Coop   27
Jellyfish   29
The Wasp   30
The Dismal Swamp   31
Amputee   32
The Chopping Block   33
The Water Witch   34
The Lost Fisherman   35

Part Three

January Thaw   39
The Icehouse   40
The Well   41
Fishing the Newfound   42
Canoe   43
June Twenty-first   44
Indian Trail   45
Leaving the Station   47
A Certain Providence   48
Brothers   49
The Saturday Night Fights   50
Houses We Lived In   51
The Ritual   53

Part One

A WINTER WITHOUT SNOW

In a winter without snow
how do we know the deer
have crossed the hard fields at night.

In a winter without snow
there's no white to glaze the sun,
gray on the hill at dawn—

no steam from the ice, no
sign of the stream underneath.
No hush in the woods, only the bone

rattle of branches as the cold
wind rises, the skeletal
clicking of sticks.

BACK ROAD

Winter mornings
driving past
I'd see these kids
huddled like grouse
in the plowed ruts
in front of their shack
waiting for the bus,
three small children
bunched against the drifts
rising behind them.

This morning
I slowed to wave
and the smallest,
a stick of a kid
draped in a coat,
grinned and raised
his red, raw hand,
the snowball
packed with rock
aimed at my face.

THE SNOW MAN

At night he changes hats,
taps his cane on the window,
a signal to your wife
who climbs down the ladder.

The wind, you say, the wind,
and go back to your novel,
a mystery, the perfect crime:
an icicle for a dagger.

In the dark, branches moan
under the weight of snow.
Your wife's hands are cold,
her lips, cracked and bleeding.

LOUIS B. RUSSELL

Louis B. Russell, a shop teacher from Indianapolis, died Wednesday after living for more than six years with a transplanted heart—longer than anyone else in history. . . . he had received the heart of a 17-year-old boy killed in a hunting accident.—The Associated Press

At night
he'd lie in bed
listening
to his new heart thump,
the blood pumping like strong legs
in a race
around the body's track,
its quick steps the echo
of his own young heart
as he reached for her hand
years ago,
that first kiss.

And falling asleep
he'd dream of the rifle, lifting it
to his cheek,
his heart wild with death:
his first buck
square in the crosshairs
as he squeezes forever the blue steel
of the trigger,
his own head in another's sights
exploding like a melon
under the blood-bright cap.

Suddenly awake,
he'd listen for hours to the clock's tick
quick as a sprinter's breath,
its bright circle of numbers
grinning in the dark,
and think
of the shop class he'd teach tomorrow,
the powerful young men,
hammers
tight in their fists.

STRAY

A dog I have never seen
howls each night
outside my window.

He has no body,
no shadow to track him by
in the dark, nothing
to hurl a rock at.

I have snuck out in slippers,
waited by bones for hours
in the cool night,
each picked clean as stars
when I woke, shivering.

For evidence the pound
needs more than a voice—
the breed, a tuft of fur—
will not answer after five
as if dogs in the dark
did not exist.

But each night
as I drift into dream
gripping a stone,
I know he'll call,
that howl
hollow as a bowl.

THE TONGUE

Love lizard, slug
of disgust,
the maker of music and mutes—
no wonder we never
put knives in our mouths.

Cross-eyed,
I can barely see its tip,
that little jewel of spit
on the end of my nose.
Blessed is he
who like the dog
has a tongue he can see.

A little river
runs through the middle,
a channel where vowels
splash and blow bubbles.
Afraid of the water
the consonants
catcall from shore.

Before wine,
Keats, it's said,
peppered his tongue,
its tiny stems
wet with red, tasting
the sugars of grape,
the coughed clots from his lungs.

TOAD

The mad uncle
nobody loves but the children.
How they squeal as he dances
hatless
in the rain.

The frog is a prince,
elegant
in his emerald jacket,
the toad, a jester,
his coat of warts,
brown motley.

Once, before time,
the toad had a beautiful voice,
sang all evening
in the grass—
sang so sweetly that birds
pecked the music from his throat.

All the songs of birds
are the toad's
hopping at the feet of kids
for laughs,
the old soft-shoe.

THE DUMP PICKERS

On Sundays
carting my trash to the dump
I'd see them swarming
the piles like gnats,
a whole family of pickers
straight from Mass:
Dad's suit, white
as the noon sky, Junior
in a polka-dot tie—
in bright, patent leathers
his small, pale sister.

From the highest of piles
Mother shouted orders
through a paper cup,
the men hurrying under
her red, high heels,
dragging metal to the pickup,
the little girl giggling,
spinning on her toes
through the blowing paper
like a dancer, a little twist
of wind in the dust.

THE APPLE

So this is the fruit that made us all human.
So this is the fruit we reached for and got.
So this is the fruit that ripens in autumn.

‡

Cezanne,
I envy your eye.
Knowing roundness,
you put an apple in a bowl,
curve into curve
like lovers.

Mother,
you sliced the green ones for pie,
steaming like morning on the sill.

Doctor,
the apple I eat to keep you away
is the shape, the weight of a heart.

‡

Long before the child, reaching up to pick,
before the ladder in the branches,
long before the tree, full in our yard,
a farmer rests
in the shade of his team.

Their dark sides shine.
In summer's last heat,
in the field's long work,

the apple he's saved
is cold on his teeth.

‡

Shine an apple on your pants.
Make the apple genie dance.

Rub him, rub him, into life.
Ask him for a pretty wife.

And for children I'd ask next,
talismans for the witch's hex.

One more wish is all that's left.
Beg him for eternal breath.

‡

Quartered,
a seed rocks
in each tiny cradle.

Like blood,
in the air an apple
rusts.

SPLITTING WOOD

When I lift my ax,
this fist on the end of a stick,
bring it thumping down
on the stump of an oak,
a door in the earth opens.

I step down into darkness,
mold and cellar musk.

The grub grins from his perch.

I hear the roots sucking
like hearts.

A furnace burns at the end of a shadow —
this dark pantry of heat!

Hello, bone,
sweet tooth of the dog.
And you, acorn,
the squirrel's dried fruit.

Warm here
below the frost line
I am brother to the mole,
the bear
wheezing all winter in his cave.

THE NEST

Found in the limbs by my son
walking the wind in the apple
the reach and hold of his climbing
the fluttering down of leaves

Held in his palm to the house
a hollow of woven reeds
of hair from the rubbings of deer
skin from the shed of a snake

Set by his bed on the bureau
by the wash of ocean in shells
the husk of a locust still singing
the silent horn of a snail

Heard in his sleep as song
a bird as bright as blood
pecking the breath from blossoms
to feed the beaks of its young

FALLING TO SLEEP

At night's ledge,
the mind frays.

The body,
heavy climber,

that sudden twitch.
Slipping, slipping—

darkness,
a rotted branch.

FLYING HOME

I

Stepping from the cab
I leap a puddle to the sidewalk,
holding tight a bag of grapefruit
brighter than the sun.
November in Florida:
the day is dark and thick.
My grandfather,
who kept us all in shoes as kids
and mailed galoshes every fall, is dead.

sixty years we were married
so short   so short

I wait in line with my bags
and remember the weight
of my grandmother's arm,
holding her yesterday at the funeral:
that soft dimpled flesh.
They pack my fruit
in a special crate.

sixty years   so short

Her white face was powdered pink.
In the sun that tried to shine,
I noticed
she is nearly bald and wears a wig.

sixty years of happiness
so short

I hurry aboard
and search for a seat
At lunch yesterday,
five of us sat at a table for six.

17

II

The stewardess
brings today's paper
and smiles
like an undertaker.

I order a drink,
a double,
and the news begins to spin.

Flying through the air
with the greatest of ease
having to pee
at ten thousand feet.

sixty years   sixty years
so short

Drunk in my seat
I stare out the window
for my grandfather
knowing he's here,
in the light,
and fall asleep.

III

From the bright, pure air
we drop into dark weather.

I sit next to the exit,
terrified of landings.

His bronze casket hovers
at the earth like the sun.

Home in just three hours!
so short   so short

We close our eyes
and the wheels touch.

Part Two

THE BOTTLE

As I pull the long cork
a glassblower in Venice,
tube in hand,
takes a deep breath.

When I whistle
at the bottle's lip,
round as any mouth,
he whistles back,

by a window wipes
the fire from his eyes.
On the canal, from the sea,
a message floats past.

Could it be
from my friend Jim
who built a ship in a bottle,
worked for weeks with sticks?

No one's seen him since.
He climbed aboard and left
not knowing in this magic glass
the genie's breath, the wind.

THE AFFAIR

Into the party on a trapeze
she uses no net.
The air around her is filled
with jugglers' bright rings.
Of all the girls you've ever met
she looks best in leopard skin.

But wait—
for her next trick,
she swallows a sword of fire.
Clever girl,
riding your boredom bareback.

With the flash of a smile
she stuffs your wife, your kids,
into a tall black hat
and pulls herself out instead.
"Yes," you cry, "Yes!"
and she saws you in half.

THE SKULL

My neighbor, a doctor, keeps a skull
in his study over his books perched there
like a raven, a real human skull
complete with filled, yellow teeth,
its cracked jaw clamped shut like some fat lady's
desperate to lose weight. With shelves
for shoulders, it just sits there
collecting dust on its shellacked, bald top,
my neighbor's four kids and delicious wife
watched by those hollow sockets each day.
"Jay," I finally asked, "why do you keep
that awful gargoyle up there anyway?"
My neighbor smiled one of those weird,
faraway surgeon's smiles and handed
me the head saying, "Hold it to your ear
and you can hear the ocean."

MUG SHOT

There are two convicts loose
from the state pen
six miles from here,
lifers, the news says,
rape and murder.

We post the cat on the porch,
bolt the door
and ready the kids for bed.

In the shower my daughter
almost four
sings like a rock star,
fogging the mirror with song.

I knock, to hurry her along,
but she doesn't answer,
the shower a heavy drummer.

I knock again and see
those faces on the screen,
that stare, the chipped grin
rising on the mirror, through the steam.

THE COOP

For years I couldn't eat chicken
or eggs
and grew sick at the thought
of which came first.
I knew.
In the coop
the red hens kicked and squawked,
beat the low roof
as I grabbed for their legs
on the roost.
I was nine,
man enough
to carry the chickens out,
to lay them on the block
for my father's ax,
the wind of their wings
against my legs.
We were saving money,
my father said,
at his old man's farm every summer
bringing home chickens for the freezer.
And save we did
since I wouldn't eat:
the wet stench of feathers
in the steaming buckets;
yellow spots of fat
on the bumped flesh;
and in my hand
from reaching in
one plucked hen
where my mother would stuff
onions and crusts
for Sunday dinner,

a half-formed egg.
No shell,
just a soft, damp sack,
like what I felt between
my boy's legs,
and as warm.

JELLYFISH

All pulse,
an eye that never closes.

With each milky billow
you shiver in a warm bay.

The sea washes over you.

You see your father,
his sweaty back,
on your mother,

sperm
beating blindly
through the salt dark.

THE WASP

Every spring a moaning,
the wasp's song
from its hut in a crack—

the crone at her wheel,
in her dark shawl,
humming—

a widow's lullaby
as she mends the larva's wrap,
needle dipping.

THE DISMAL SWAMP

Off Highway 7
in North Carolina
where the road tunnels
through webs of moss
strangling the branches,
logs rise
from dead water
where the bass fans
with her thick tail
the fertilized eggs,
a cloud drifting into
her flat, blank eyes:
the black water shattering
and the duckling, its
yellow beak gaping,
swallowed whole
as iron-gilled she hits
at anything: duck,
copperhead, oar—
defending the young
she devours when born.

AMPUTEE

One would toss,
the other, catch—

so easy together,
lovely to watch.

The right arm lost,
he reaches to touch,

still feeling its weight,
the right with the left.

THE CHOPPING BLOCK

In its center, a stain,
the dark core of maple—
a knot of dried blood,
a little twist of pain.

Here, the emperor laid his head,
loosened his linen collar.
Twiddling through centuries,
the chopped thumbs of thieves.

On this bull's-eye
I put a log to split, heft
the bright blade, hear
the fat hen squawk.

In my darkest dreams I climb
the hill with my son. His curls
spill on the block. Knife raised,
I stare at the sky.

This block is so old
moss grows on its side.
Look into this compass, sailor.
Weep, for you are lost.

THE WATER WITCH

A curse and he's there,
dryness come for a drink
singing his song of thirst,
the wind like dust in his veins.

For a stick he takes
a snake from a sack,
holds the halves of its tongue,
walking your land for water.

At the spot where in your dreams
you shoveled a grave,
the tail quivers, drives downward
through the gnawed heart.

"Drink," he says, knowing your thirst,
the sweating cup in his hand.
In your throat it is cold and good,
with a taste of salt, like tears.

THE LOST FISHERMAN

Waist-deep,
you've seen no one
since noon.

Dusk.
The fog upstream
follows you down.

You keep
carefully ahead,
the pines thick
on both banks.

Heat lightning.

Suddenly
someone else
is on the river.

His white eyes are watching.

You wave,
He nods.

You cast, wait
and look back.

He is gone.

You have stayed too late.
Deep in the river,
the white silence of fog.

Part Three

JANUARY THAW

This is the time of forgiveness,
when your father
would bend down to you
just before sleep,
the breath of his kiss
the warmth of this breeze
as you walk the slope
behind the house,
the land you'd forgotten
under the drifts:
how the stones,
steaming with light,
steady the earth
in the melting snow.

THE ICEHOUSE

Where the puckerbush snags your lure
along the west edge of the lake is where
the icehouse stood, black with wet
in the sweat of summer, glistening all winter.
I cast to the pilings rising like masts
from the water, from the mist, and see the breath
of horses dragging blades, their muscled thighs—
hear the men in rubber aprons, slick as fish,
cursing the blocks, the cold, prodding each piece
with their spikes to the shore. All afternoon
the clank, the hiss of the belt lifting
chunk after chunk through the winter light
to its dark bed of hay in this place
of black timber, this ship rising like a dream
through the sand, through the rock, its hold
cradling silver, cooling the fruit of summer.

THE WELL

The mystery of water underground,
the dark stream where the dead kneel
cupping their white hands,
splashing the stillness from their eyes.

I drop a stone in ours to hear
if there's water for the children's bath.
And if it's dry, no sound—the pebble
a star, falling through the night.

Here, a rope once hung, a bucket
on its noose. Here, the cattle gathered
summer evenings at the trough,
their dull heads bowed.

No one fishes this hole, or ever did,
though in the cold, moonless pools
fins move through the dark, deep
in the ground, where spawning begins.

FISHING THE NEWFOUND

Happy, creel heavy with trout,
I climb the steep bank to the pines
to wait out the storm coming on,
its sudden light flaming the river,
logs, torched canoes in the dark.

In a coat of needles, sweet with pitch,
I listen to the drops puckering pools
like fish after flies
and reach in my creel for a trout,
the firm spine and yolk orange belly,
my fingers rich with its slime like spit, sperm.

All around me
red-winged blackbirds
singing the sun coming back,
the yellow bells of flowers I cannot name
and crushed fern at my feet.

I step out alone, alone
on the bank, the world glistening
before mosquitoes, before time,
before the rib was cut from my side.

CANOE

A swallow
skimming the pond at dusk,
how it tilts to the water
the curve of its wing.

I push off from shore,
casting for trout.
The dip of paddle, the silence,
nothing but ripples of breeze.

Imagine his hands,
the edge of his blade,
who hollowed this bird from a log.

JUNE TWENTY-FIRST

My mother's cigarette flares and fades,
the steady pulse of a firefly,
on the patio under the chestnut.

The next door neighbors are over.
My father, still slender, is telling a joke:
laughter jiggles in everyone's drinks.

On his hour's reprieve from sleep,
my little brother dances
in the sprinkler's circle of water.

At fourteen, I'm too old
to run naked with my brother,
too young to laugh with my father.

I stand there with my hands in my pockets.
The sun refuses to set,
bright as a penny in a loafer.

INDIAN TRAIL

The career of our play brought us through the dark muddy lanes behind the houses where we ran the gauntlets of the rough tribes. — James Joyce

This is not a poem about Indians.
I know nothing about them,
being from the suburbs of Boston
where the last Indians were probably burned
with the witches at Salem.
We lived on a narrow street
in my grandparents' old brown house;
it had bright shutters
and a large front porch
where, during a scrap, my best friend Henry
once clouted me on the head
with my own cowboy pistol.

In the smoke of late afternoons my grandfather
would lead Henry and me
down our street of gray lawns,
past the voices on the screened porches
whispering like priests, guiding us safely
by Mrs. Burner's pet mutt growling like Cerberus,
to the park's tennis courts
and the small patch of woods beside them.
Here, where the new high school
was later to be built,
he'd show us the path
where Indians danced all night
in our minds, their painted faces
flashing like jack-o'-lanterns by the fire.
Into this first world
we ran with drawn guns,
or, when Henry couldn't come,
as my grandfather waited,
I'd walk the dark trail terrified,
a pilgrim wanting to make peace.

I seldom saw Henry after he hit me
and later
after my father came back from the war,
we moved away.
The old house was eventually sold
and my grandfather,
always at ease with the darkness,
we laid to rest in Florida,
where, they say,
there are still real Indians
deep in the winding Everglades.

LEAVING THE STATION

The tug of starting.
I watch the windows
on the other track,
the flash of their lights
through the station's dark.
We back into evening,
my face on the glass.

The car is warm
and in its rocking
I hear my grandfather,
long since dead,
shuffling cards,
the soft applause
of their falling together.

This is his last trip south.
He knows he is dying
but can't remember the rules
or whose deal.
He shuffles, restacks,
shuffles again,
nodding his head with the rails.

A CERTAIN PROVIDENCE

Fall. At my doorstep I find
hurled there like the paper
lying beside it, a sparrow,
its twig of a neck snapped,
a bubble of blood on its beak.
I lift it by its wishbone
of a wing and see as I do
in the storm-door window
I put up last week
a sky without wind, fresh
and deep as water in wells,
orchards of bright red leaves
etched against its blue,
see this bird, gliding
with a song into this world
of glass sky and tree.

BROTHERS

9-year-old Michael Wilson was killed while feeding his 9-month-old brother, Timothy, in the dining room of their single-story frame house. The helicopter plunged through the roof about 5:30 P.M.
—The Norfolk *Virginian-Pilot*

Early this Monday morning
as the sharp, chopping blades
of the traffic copter
whirred over the dozing suburbs,
I thought of you,
Michael Wilson,
who, when called in
last Friday at five,
laid down your mitt and bat
to feed your only brother,
the brother you had always wanted,
the brother born too late
to play ball with.

In the dining room
of the flat, frame house
you bounced him on your knee
as a father might
and fed him for your mother,
holding him close
on your own small lap
as he sucked the warm milk.

At 5:26
the random ax fell,
breaking your body like a branch.
In the rubble echoing with his cries,
they found your brother alive,
swaddled
in a wreath of crushed bone.

THE SATURDAY NIGHT FIGHTS

In our basement playroom
my father would pull
my brother's toy rocker
closer to our Zenith,
pounding its thin wooden sides
to get a clear picture.

In a fourteen inch
badly blurred ring,
Sugar Ray and Basilio
slugged each other's eyes shut
every last night of the week.

Rocker creaking, about to break,
my father groaned with each
sock to the jaw,
hollering "fix"
whenever a knockout
ended the evening early.

It was always too quickly.
Quiet,
he climbed the long stairs
to kids and work, the white dot
behind him in the dark.

HOUSES WE LIVED IN

I

The first was dark brown.
We had a big yard then
but my father, a soldier, was never home.

Always, in the living room
the heavy drapes were drawn.
In their shadows my grandmother's jade chows
guarded, like gargoyles, her teakwood tables.
Built like Buddha, she worshipped the Orient.

The kitchen was pure white.
A crucifix cloaked with palms
hung by the clock, next to the table.
The ice box hummed its hymn.
At breakfast my grandfather,
his right ear a suction cup,
listened for news of the war.

II

The second was the yellow of sun.
I watched my father, high on the ladder,
his brush filling in the sky.

The attic was a turret, my secret,
where draped in my father's uniform,
I pledged to keep the Reds away.

Then once, while looking for his medals
in the bureau in their bedroom,
I found a slick, round, cold piece of rubber.

III

The third had no color at all,
stark as stone in the hot sun of June
when I first came home from college.

We sat in the den,
our words twisted by gin
and the war I wouldn't fight.

At dinner that night,
the last word slipped like a knife:
the blood of the meat pooled on our plates.

IV

This is my own,
a deep blue house near the ocean.

My cat walks the battlements of our picket fence.
My wife raises fennel in the window box.
My son sings in his swing from the maple.

The long war is nearly over.
In the fall I'll go hunting with my father.

THE RITUAL

The first night of frost
we all have our chores,
the children in the garden
picking tomatoes
hard as apples;
in their mother's hands,
the final flowers.
I hood in plastic
what plants I can
and as the wind stills
lug in wood,
stacking oak against the dark
the clearest night of the year.

The first night of frost
we go to bed early,
the children at their prayers,
in the darkness
their soft words;
my wife in her slippers
going up the stairs.
I open the window
and smell the air,
hear as I hold her
in the warmth of our bed
a dog bark, far off,
under the stars.

PITT POETRY SERIES
Ed Ochester, General Editor

Dannie Abse, *Collected Poems*
Claribel Alegria, *Flowers from the Volcano*
Jack Anderson, *Toward the Liberation of the Left Hand*
Jon Anderson, *Death & Friends*
Jon Anderson, *In Sepia*
Jon Anderson, *Looking for Jonathan*
John Balaban, *After Our War*
Michael Benedikt, *The Badminton at Great Barrington; Or, Gustave Mahler & the Chattanooga Choo-Choo*
Michael Burkard, *Ruby for Grief*
Kathy Callaway, *Heart of the Garfish*
Lorna Dee Cervantes, *Emplumada*
Robert Coles, *A Festering Sweetness: Poems of American People*
Leo Connellan, *First Selected Poems*
Fazil Hüsnü Dağlarca, *Selected Poems*
Norman Dubie, *Alehouse Sonnets*
Stuart Dybek, *Brass Knuckles*
Odysseus Elytis, *The Axion Esti*
John Engels, *Blood Mountain*
John Engels, *Signals from the Safety Coffin*
Brendan Galvin, *The Minutes No One Owns*
Brendan Galvin, *No Time for Good Reasons*
Gary Gildner, *Digging for Indians*
Gary Gildner, *First Practice*
Gary Gildner, *Nails*
Gary Gildner, *The Runner*
Bruce Guernsey, *January Thaw*
Mark Halperin, *Backroads*
Patricia Hampl, *Woman Before an Aquarium*
Michael S. Harper, *Song: I Want a Witness*
John Hart, *The Climbers*
Samuel Hazo, *Blood Rights*
Samuel Hazo, *Once for the Last Bandit: New and Previous Poems*
Samuel Hazo, *Quartered*
Gwen Head, *Special Effects*
Gwen Head, *The Ten Thousandth Night*
Milne Holton and Graham W. Reid, eds., *Reading the Ashes: An Anthology of the Poetry of Modern Macedonia*
Milne Holton and Paul Vangelisti, eds., *The New Polish Poetry: A Bilingual Collection*
David Huddle, *Paper Boy*

Shirley Kaufman, *The Floor Keeps Turning*
Shirley Kaufman, *From One Life to Another*
Shirley Kaufman, *Gold Country*
Ted Kooser, *Sure Signs: New and Selected Poems*
Larry Levis, *Wrecking Crew*
Jim Lindsey, *In Lieu of Mecca*
Tom Lowenstein, tr., *Eskimo Poems from Canada and Greenland*
Archibald MacLeish, *The Great American Fourth of July Parade*
Peter Meinke, *The Night Train and The Golden Bird*
Peter Meinke, *Trying to Surprise God*
Judith Minty, *In the Presence of Mothers*
James Moore, *The New Body*
Carol Muske, *Camouflage*
Leonard Nathan, *Dear Blood*
Leonard Nathan, *Holding Patterns*
Kathleen Norris, *The Middle of the World*
Sharon Olds, *Satan Says*
Gregory Pape, *Border Crossings*
Thomas Rabbitt, *Exile*
Ed Roberson, *Etai-Eken*
Ed Roberson, *When Thy King Is A Boy*
Eugene Ruggles, *The Lifeguard in the Snow*
Dennis Scott, *Uncle Time*
Herbert Scott, *Groceries*
Richard Shelton, *Of All the Dirty Words*
Richard Shelton, *Selected Poems, 1969-1981*
Richard Shelton, *You Can't Have Everything*
Gary Soto, *The Elements of San Joaquin*
Gary Soto, *The Tale of Sunlight*
Gary Soto, *Where Sparrows Work Hard*
David Steingass, *American Handbook*
Tomas Tranströmer, *Windows & Stones: Selected Poems*
Alberta T. Turner, *Learning to Count*
Alberta T. Turner, *Lid and Spoon*
Chase Twichell, *Northern Spy*
Constance Urdang, *The Lone Woman and Others*
Cary Waterman, *The Salamander Migration and Other Poems*
Bruce Weigl, *A Romance*
David P. Young, *The Names of a Hare in English*
David P. Young, *Sweating Out the Winter*